I0791152

Erika Figula - Ferenc Margitics -
Zsuzsa Pauwlik

The Outsider
as Bystander Role
in School Bullying

The Outsider as Bystander Role
in School Bullying

Authored by: Erika Figula Ph.D., Ferenc
Margitics Ph.D., Zsuzsa Pauwlik Ph.D.
(figula.erika@nye.hu)

Published by: Ervin Kery
(editor@kery.org)

(c)2020 Erika Figula Ph.D.

ISBN: 9781654411428

CONTENTS

Preface

Our research group established by the Department of Psychology at the College of Nyíregyháza investigates the phenomena of school bullying and harassment. The term 'school bullying covers the behaviour where the aggressive act has no obvious cause (non-reactive aggression).

Our research focuses on the question that among upper school primary school students and high school students what kind of background factors may stand in the background of aggressive attitude and behavior patterns of school bullying (bully, victim, bystander, intervener participant and helper participant). During our research, we charted those background factors, which help to understand the process of the development of bully, victim, participant and bystander behavior patterns, as well as they allow the development of the options of efficient mental hygiene.

In this book we examined the relation between **outsider as bystander behavior pattern** in school bullying and certain parental treatments (such as; parental solicitude, parental overprotection and parental restriction). We wanted to find an answer to the question: what kind of temperament and character traits the students have, who become bullies through school bullying and what their typical emotional reactions are.

In our research we used the following instruments: the Questionnaire on School Bullying, the Hungarian adaptation of Goch's Family Socializational, the Hungarian adaptation of the Parental Bonding Instrument, the Hungarian version of Cloninger's Temperament and Character Inventory, the Hungarian version of Differential Emotions Scale, The Hungarian version of Weismann's Scale of Dysfunctional Attitudes and The Hungarian adaptation of the Folkman–Lazarus Conflict Solving Questionnaire.

Introduction

Bystanders are the individuals who observe bullying, are present in the vast majority of bullying incidents. (Swearer and Hymel, 2015).

According to research by O'Connell and colleagues (1999) the bullying episodes on the school show that most of the time children stand by and passively observe violence (54%).

The main roles of bystanders include reinforcer, assistant, outsider, and defender. The bystander may take the role of outsider; in this role, the bystander has no direct involvement in the bullying incident but acts as a silent approver through inaction. (Salmivalli et al. 1996).

Bullying has been most often examined from the victim and aggressor perspectives. In recent years, there is a growing body of research examining bullying as role of bystanders in the process. (Raboteg-Saric and Bartakovic, 2019) Through school bullying, the passive bystanders' attitude is mainly positive but they do not undertake openly that they like aggression. They do not take an active role but they encourage harassment and aggression (Olweus 1997).

Research indicate that bystanders seldom act in ways that support the victims (Craig et al., 2000)

According to Thornberg and Jungert (2013) research the adolescents see the wrongness of bullying, they may remain as passive bystanders because they do not believe that they are capable of intervening effectively.

According Tani et al. (2003) personality traits, contribute to children's typical behaviour in bullying situations. Defenders of the victim exhibited the highest levels of friendliness (agreeableness) relative to their peers, while introversion and independence characterised outsiders.

According to our research in Hungarian primary and secondary school we found bystander behavior pattern less typical of boys, in case of the primary school students it was the third, in case of the high school students it was the fourth most dominant behavior pattern, from the components of which keeping one's distance was also the most dominant in the case of boys. (Margitics et. al, 2019).

METHODOLOGY

Participants

Factors of Family Socialization

In the study 647 (301 girls, 346 boys) primary and high school students took part. The distribution of the sample according to schools was the following:

> Primary school, upper school: 293 participants (140 girls, 150 boys)
> High school: 354 participants (161 girls, 193 boys)

The sample according to age:

> Primary school, upper school: 13,2 year old
> High school: 16,7 year old

Temperament and Character

The data for the research project were gathered from students of secondary grammar schools.

341 students participated in the project,

195 women and 146 men.

The average age was 16,4 years (standard deviation: 1,4).

Emotions, Attitudes and Coping Mechanisms

The data for the research project were gathered from students of primary education at elementary schools and secondary grammar schools.

706 students participated in the project, 397 women and 309 men.

The average age was 15,2 years (standard deviation: 1,7).

Measures

Factors of Family Socialization

We applied two different questionnaires.

The Hungarian adaptation of Goch's Family Socializational Questionnaire (Goch, 1998, Sallay & Dabert, 2002).

The questionnaire describes the following dimensions of family socialization:

> - type of the family atmosphere (rule-oriented family atmosphere, conflict-oriented family atmosphere),
> - breeding target (breeding for autonomy, autonomy as a target of breeding, breeding for conformity, conformity as a breeding target),
> - educational attitudes (consistent educational attitude, manipulative educational attitude, inconsistent educational attitude)
> - educational style (supporting educational style, punishing educational style).

The Hungarian adaptation of the Parental Bonding Instrument (Tóth and Gervai, 1999).

The questionnaire has three main scales: love and care, overprotection, and restriction, applied separately to the mother and the father.

Temperament and Character

The Hungarian version of Cloninger's Temperament and Character Inventory (Rózsa et al. 2005)

The main scales of the measure describe four temperament and three character dimensions:

- ➢ The temperament-scales are novelty seeking, harm avoidance, reward dependence, persistence
- ➢ The character-scales are self-directedness, cooperativeness, self-transcendence.

Emotions

Hungarian version of Differentional Emotions Scale (Oláh, 2005).

Izard (1971) developed Differentional Emotions Scale in order to differentiate between the basic emotions. The inventory is suitable for examining the ability of experiencing certain basic emotions as a permanent characteristic feature. With the help of a frequency scale it examines how often the basic emotions appear.

Differential Emotions Scale consists of a scale identifying ten basic emotions. The questionnaire describes the following fundamental emotions:

> Trait of Interest
> Trait of Enjoyment
> Trait of Surprise
> Trait of Distress
> Trait of Anger
> Trait of Disgust
> Trait of Contempt
> Trait of Fear
> Trait of Shame
> Trait of Guilt
> Trait of Anxiety

The Hungarian adaptation of the questionnaire was done by Oláh (2005), who found the reliability of the scales good (Cronbach-alpha=0,49-0,76).

Attitudes

The Hungarian version of Weismann's Scale of Dysfunctional Attitudes (Weisman and Beck, 1979, Kopp, 1994).

The scale included question of following attitudes:

> desire for external appraisal, need for affections, performance orientation, perfectionism, rightful and intensive requirements towards the environment, omnipotence (intensive altruism) and external control - autonomy.

Coping Mechanisms

The Hungarian adaptation of the Folkman–Lazarus Conflict Solving Questionnaire (Kopp, 1994).

The questionnaire contains 22 items and is used to reveal the behaviour of individuals in difficult situations. Respondents use a four-grade scale for each answer, from "entirely irrelevant" to "fully relevant."

Folkman and Lazarus arranged conflict-solving strategies into problem-based and emotion-based categories. The surveys conducted by Kopp and Skrabski (1995) confirmed the validity of this categorization. They found three problem-driven, three emotion-driven and one support-seeking factor. These are the following:

> Problem analysis
> Cognitive restructuring
> Conformance
> Emotion-driven action
> Seeking emotional balance
> Retrieval
> Call for help
> A summary indicator of the problem-driven coping strategy
> A summary indicator of the emotion-driven coping strategy

Problem-driven coping strategies (problem analysis, cognitive re-structuring, conformance) measure the ability of the individual to analyse the problem, to influence the reasons and to obtain control over it. It also measures the ability of cognitive re-structuring.

The second three emotion-driven coping strategies (emotion-driven action, seeking emotional equilibrium, retrieval) and call for help will come forward when the individual is not satisfactorily familiar with the problem or feels unable to obtain control over the situation.

The Examination of School Bullying

The Questionnaire on School Bullying (Figula et al., 2019).

For purposes of identifying patterns of behaviour in school bullying, the School Bullying Questionnaire was used.

The 70 items of SBQ offers options of "almost never," "sometimes," "often," "almost always," and investigates the phenomena of school bullying and abuse in everyday life through five dimensions.

With the exception of "intervener participant" scale, all dimensions include further subscales. (Chart 1).

Scales and Subscales	Item	Cronbach-alfa
Victim Scale	**33**	**0,847**
Cognitive Subscale (Conscious recognition of abuse and processing it)	15	0,877
Affective Subscale (The emotional effect of abuse)	12	0,864
Somatic reaction (Somatic reaction to abuse / acting out)	3	0,758
Lack of Social Support Subscale (Lack of acceptance in class community)	3	0,814
Intervener Participant Scale	**3**	**0,784**
Helper Participant Scale	**8**	**0,753**

Intervening to Pacify Subscale	3	0,748
Intervening to Ask for Help Subscale	2	0,778
Affective Subscale (Inner tension as a result of witnessing aggression)	3	0,749
Bystander Scale	**9**	**0,768**
Keeping Distance Subscale	6	0,758
Fear Subscale	3	0,743
Bully Scale	**17**	**0,843**
Physical Aggression Subscale	4	0,845
Verbal Aggression Subscale	5	0,849
Exclusion Subscale	5	0,754
Advantage From Attack Subscale	3	0,768

Chart 1. Scales and Subscales of the School Bullying Questionnaire

The Criteria of Compiling the Research Group and the Control Group

When we formed the test groups, we considered the results scored on the scales of Questionnaire on School Bullying, which examines the behavior patterns of school bullying, within this, which quartiles the tested people got into.

Those students got into the group of students becoming bystander during school bullying, who fell into the fourth quartile of the sample on the basis of the results scored on the Bystander Scale.

Those students got into the group of students not becoming bystander during school bullying, who fell into the first quartile of the sample on the basis of the results scored on the Bystander Scale.

Results

Factors of Family Socialization

The structure of Family Socialization factors

With the help of second-rate factor analysis (varimax rotation) we examined the patterns of parental educational dimensions, its underlying structure (during the study- according to general practice- not less than 0,4 (factor gravity) rotated factors were taken into account (Chart 2).

Dimensions of Parental Bonding	Factor 1	Factor 2	Factor 3	Factor 4
Rule oriented family atmosphere	0,641			
Conflict oriented family atmosphere		0,730		
Manipulative educational attitude		0,670		
Inconsistent educational attitude		0,758		

Consistent educational attitude	**0,662**			
Punishing educational style	**0,772**			
Supportive educational style			**-0,469**	
Breeding for conformity	**0,759**			
Breeding for autonomy			**-0,619**	
Maternal affection-care		**-0,595**		
Paternal affection-care		**-0,648**		
Maternal overprotection				**0,854**
Paternal overprotection				**0,878**
Maternal restriction			**0,898**	
Paternal restriction			**0,895**	

Chart 2. Second Rate Factor Analysis for the Dimensions of Parental Nurturing (l>0.4)

The analysis arranged parental educational dimension into four factors, which together explained 64,9% of the variance.

The first factor, which explains 25,2% of the variance, demonstrates rule oriented family atmosphere, which is characterized by conformity as parental educational goal and it associates with punishing educational style and consistent educational attitude.

The second factor, which explains 21,4% of the variance, demonstrates conflict oriented family atmosphere, which is characterized by conflict oriented family atmosphere, the manipulative and inconsistent educational attitude of the parents and the lack of love and care.

The third factor, which explains 10,6% of the variance, demonstrates restrictional parental treatment, which is characterized by the lack of parental support and breeding for autonomy

The fourth factor, which explains 7,7%of the variance, describes parental overprotection.

The connection between bystander behavior patterns of school bullying and parental educational effects were revealed by linear regression analysis (stepwise method: dependant variable was the bystander behavior pattern of school bullying, parental educational effects were used as predictor).

Chart 3 shows the results of linear regression analysis in case of bystander behavior pattern.

Predictor	B	t	P<
Women: $F_{totál}$=5,731; df=1/301; p<0,018			
Difference between manipulative educational attitude	0,191	2,394	0,018
Men: $F_{totál}$=16,087; df=2/346; p<0,000			
Maternal punishing educational style	0,212	4,076	0,000
Paternal manipulative educational attitude	0,187	3,607	0,000

Chart 3. Interrelationship between Parental Rearing Effects with the Behaviour Patterns of the Bystander (approved models; p<0.05)

In case of the girls, bystander behavior pattern, from the family socialization effects, only showed a significant, positive connection with the difference between the parental manipulative educational attitude, which together explained 3,6 % of the variance of bystander behavior pattern.

In case of the boys, bystander behavior pattern, from the family socialization effects, only showed a significant, positive connection with maternal punishing educational style and paternal manipulative educational attitude, which together explained 8,6 % of the variance of bystander behavior pattern.

Temperament and Character

The aim of this present chapter is to explore the connection between the bystander behavior pattern of school bullying and the temperament and character traits of personality and their constituent personality traits.

We examined what differences exist between the test groups (bystander vs. non-bystander) on the basis of the results scored on the IBystandert Scale of the Questionnaire on School Bullying examining the behavior patterns of school bullying.

Figure 1 shows the averages scored on the certain scales of Temperament and Character Inventory of bystander vs. non-bystander test groups in case of the girls.

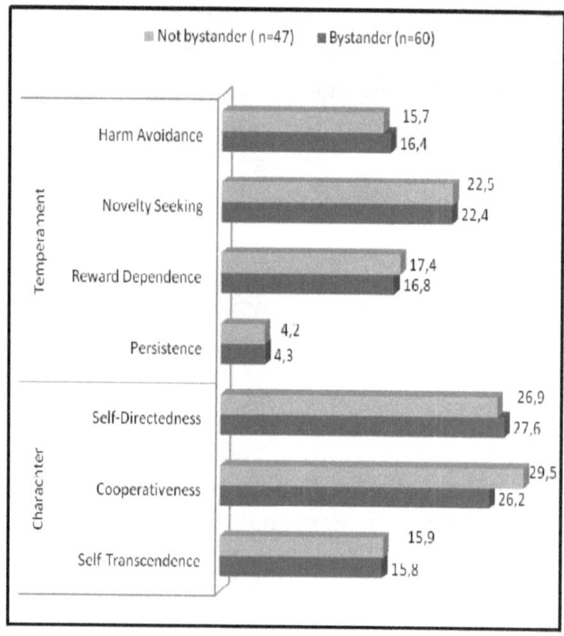

Figure 1. Averages Achieved on the Individual Scales of the Temperament and Character Inventory by Bystander Test Group vs. Non-Bystander participant Test Group (girls)

In case of the girls, also only in the area of character traits, we found significant differences between the test groups on the basis of Comparative Statistical Analysis.

From the character traits in the degree of cooperativeness was significant difference between the groups. Cooperativeness was less typical of the girls becoming bystander (t=2,229, p=0,023), than the girls not becoming bystander.

In point of temperament traits, we did not find significant differences between the groups.

Figure 2 shows the averages scored on the certain scales of Temperament and Character Inventory of bystander and not bystander control groups in case of the boys.

In case of the boys, also only in the area of character traits, we found significant differences between the test groups on the basis of Comparative Statistical Analysis.

From the character traits in the degree of cooperativeness was significant difference between the groups. Cooperativeness (t=2,198, p=0,028) was also less typical of the boys becoming bystanders, than the boys not becoming bystanders.

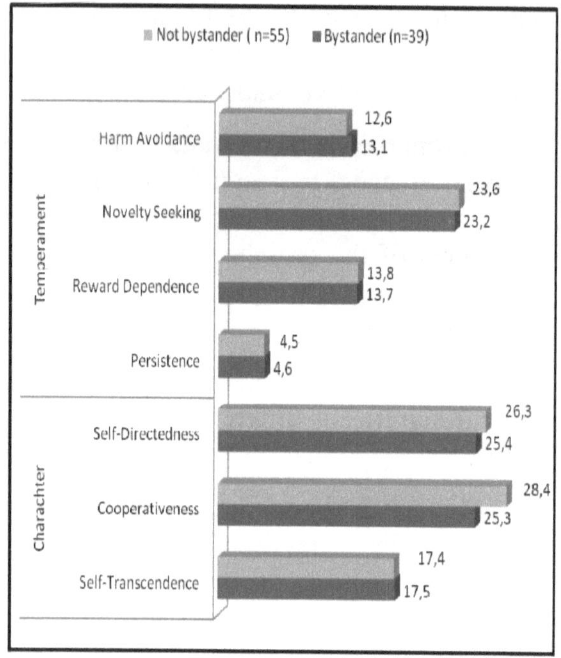

Figure 2. Averages Achieved on the Individual Scales of the Temperament and Character Inventory by Bystander Test Group vs. Non-Bystander participant Test Group (boys)

In point of temperament traits, we did not find significant differences between the groups in case of the boys either.

The connection between bystander behavior pattern of school bullying and temperament and character traits were revealed by linear regression analysis (stepwise method: dependant variable was the bystander behavior pattern of school bullying, independent variables were the certain temperament and character traits and their constituent personality traits.

Chart 4 shows the results of linear regression analysis in case of bystander behavior pattern.

Predictor	B	t	P<
Women: $F_{totál}$=4,640; df=1/195; p<0,032			
Cooperativeness	-0,153	-2,154	0,032
Men: $F_{totál}$=10,399; df=1/146; p<0,027			
Cooperativeness	-0,164	2,402	0,027

Chart 4. Correlation between Temperament and Character Features and the Behaviour Pattern of the Bystander (approved models; p<0.05)

In case of the girls, bystander behavior pattern, from the temperament an character traits and their constituent personality traits, showed a significant, negative connection only with cooperativeness, which explained 4,5 % of the variance.

In case of the boys, bystander behavior pattern, from the temperament an character traits and their constituent personality traits, showed a significant, negative connection only with cooperativeness, which explained 5,6 % of the variance.

Emotions

We examined what difference exists between the test groups in point of basic emotions on the basis of the results scored on the scales of the bystander behavior pattern' Questionnaire on School Bullying.

Figure 3 shows the averages scored on the certain scales of Differential Emotions Scale of bystander vs. not bystander control groups in case of the girls.

Comparative Statistical Analysis shows that there were significant differences between the control groups in point of more basic emotions.

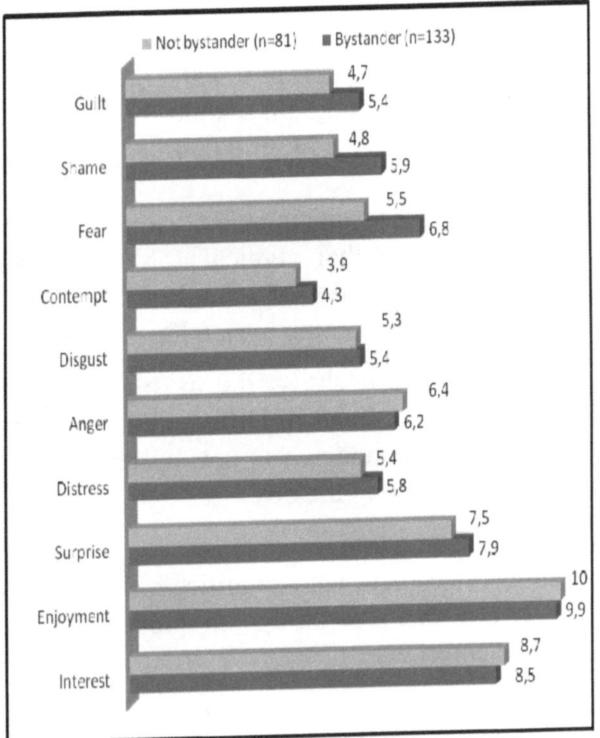

Figure 3. Averages Achieved on the Individual Scales of the Differential Emotions Scale by Bystander Test Group vs. Non-Bystander Test Group (girls)

These are the following:

- ➢ Fear (t=4,431, p<0,000)
- ➢ Shame (t=3,350, p<0,001)
- ➢ Guilt (t=2,134, p<0,034)

These results indicate that fear, shame guilt were rather typical of the girls becoming bystander of school bullying than the girls not becoming bystander.

Figure 4 shows the averages scored on the certain scales of Differential Emotions Scale of bystander vs. not bystander test groups in case of the boys.

Comparative Statistical Analysis shows that there were significant differences between the test groups in point of more basic emotions.

These are the following:

- ➢ Shame (t=4,392, p<0,000)
- ➢ Fear (t=3,881, p<0,000)
- ➢ Guilt (t=2,057, p<0,043)

These results mean that fear, shame, guilt were rather typical of the boys becoming bystander of school bullying than the boys not becoming bystander.

The connection between the bystander behavior pattern of school bullying and the basic emotions were revealed by linear regression analysis (stepwise method: dependant variable was bystander behavior pattern, basic emotions were used as predictors).

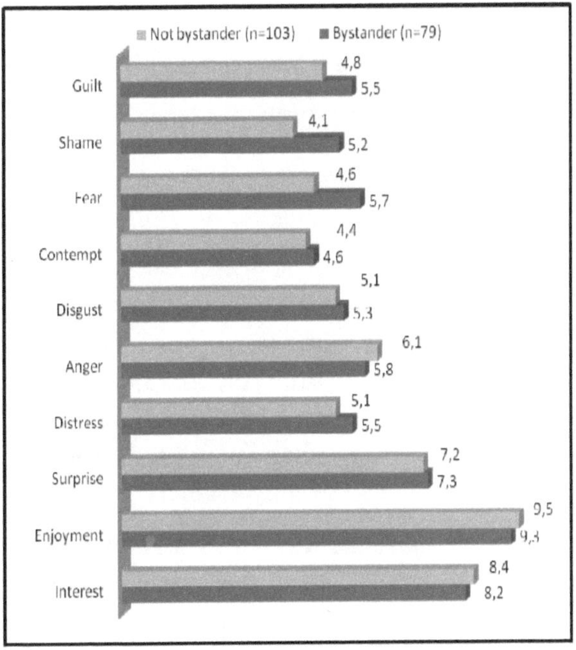

Figure 4. Averages Achieved on the Individual Scales of the Differentional Emotions Scale by Bystander Test Group vs. Non- Bystander Test Group (boys)

Chart 5 shows the results of linear regression analysis in case of bystander behavior pattern.

Predictor	B	t	P<
Women: $F_{totál}$=22,744; df=2/397; p<0,000			
Fear	0,253	5,087	0,000
Shame	0,194	4,067	0,000
Men: $F_{totál}$=14,076; df=2/309; p<0,000			
Fear	0,187	2,956	0,003
Shame	0,148	2,339	0,020

Chart 5. Relationship of Fundamental Emotions with the Behaviour Pattern of the Bystander (approved models; p<0.05)

In case of the girls, bystander behavior pattern, from the basic emotions, showed a significant, positive connection with fear and shame, which together explained 10,4 % of the variance.

In case of the boys, the bystander behavior pattern, from the basic emotions, showed a significant, positive connection also with fear and shame, which together explained 8,4 % of the variance.

These results indicate that the students becoming bystanders of school bullying – without reference to gender differences- feel fear and shame.

We also examined that what the connection is between the certain components of bystander behavior pattern (keeping one's distance, fear) and the basic emotions (linear regression, stepwise method: dependant variable is the components of bystander behavior pattern, basic emotions were used as predictors).

Chart 6 shows the revealed connections with this method.

In case of the girls, the keeping one's distance component of bystander behavior pattern, from the basic emotions, showed a significant, positive connection with contempt and fear and a negative one with anger, which together explained 9,6 % of the variance.

Predictor	B	t	P<
Keeping one's distance			
Women: F$_{totál}$=13,898; df=3/397; p<0,000			
Contempt	0,241	4,664	0,000
Fear	0,204	4,216	0,000
Anger	-0,167	-3,191	0,002
Men: F$_{totál}$=7,926; df=2/309; p<0,000			
Fear	0,204	3,628	0,000
Anger	-0,116	-2,070	0,039

Women: $F_{tot\acute{a}l}$=23,594; df=2/397; p<0,000			
Fear	0,217	6,293	0,000
Shame	0,168	3,201	0,001
Men: $F_{tot\acute{a}l}$=19,695; df=2/309; p<0,000			
Fear	0,215	3,462	0,000
Shame	0,174	2,803	0,005

Chart 6. Regression Analysis of Fundamental Emotions versus the Individual Components of the Bystander Behaviour Pattern (approved models; p<0.05)

In case of the boys, the keeping one's distance component of bystander behavior pattern, from the basic emotions, showed a significant, positive connection with also fear and a negative one with anger, which together explained 4,9 % of the variance.

In case of the girls, the fear component of bystander behavior pattern, from the basic emotions, showed a significant, positive connection with fear and shame, which together explained 21,6 % of the variance.

In case of the boys, the fear component of bystander behavior pattern, from the basic emotions, showed a significant, positive connection with also fear and shame, which together explained 20,2 % of the variance.

Attitudes

We examined what difference exists between the test groups in point of dysfunctional attitudes on the basis of the results scored on the scale of the bystander behavior pattern' Questionnaire on School Bullying.

Figure 5 shows the averages scored on the certain scales of Scale of Dysfunctional Attitudes of bystander vs. not bystander test groups in case of the girls.

Comparative Statistical Analysis shows that there were significant differences between the test groups in point of more dysfunctional attitudes.

These are the following:

- ➢ Need for affections ($t=3,639$ $p<0,000$)
- ➢ Intensive altruism ($t=3,406$, $p<0,001$)
- ➢ Rightful and intensive requirements towards the environment ($t=3,121$, $p<0,002$)

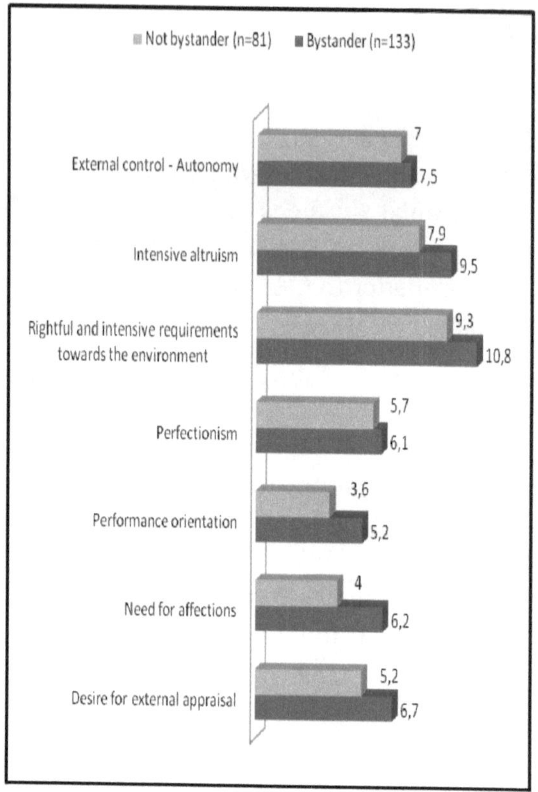

Figure 5. Averages Achieved on the Scale of Dysfunctional Attitudes by the Bystander Test Group vs. Non-Bystander Test Group (girls)

> Desire for external appraisal (t=3,002, p<0,003)
> Performance orientation (t=2,616, p<0,010)

These results indicate that need for affections, intensive altruism, intensive requirements towards the environment, desire for external appraisal, performance orientation were rather typical of the girls becoming bystanders of school bullying than the girls not becoming bystanders.

Figure 6 shows the averages scored on the certain scales of Scale of Dysfunctional Attitudes of bystander vs. not bystander test groups in case of the boys.

Comparative Statistical Analysis shows that there were significant differences between the test groups in point of only two dysfunctional attitudes. These are the following:

> Performance orientation (t=4,126, p<0,000)
> Need for affections (t=3,772 p<0,000)

These results indicate that desire for external appraisal was rather typical of the boys becoming bystanders of school bullying than the boys not becoming bystanders.

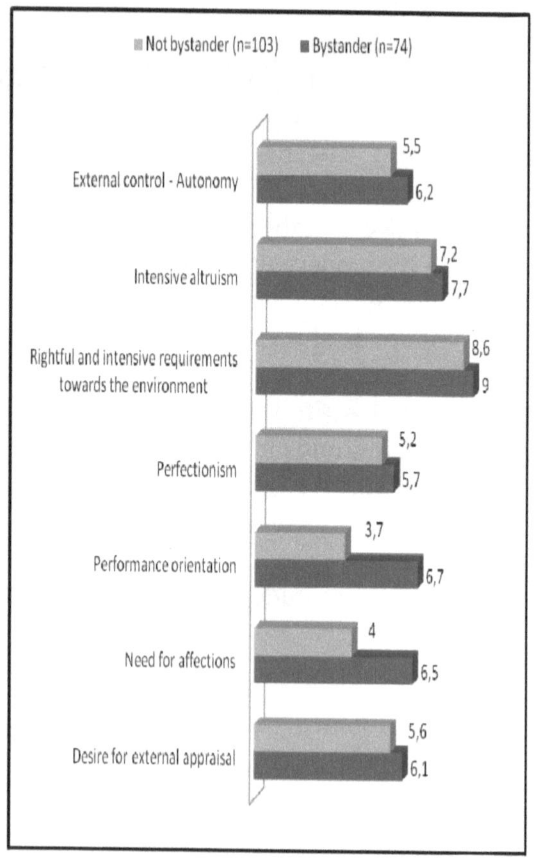

Figure 6. Averages Achieved on the Scale of Dysfunctional Attitudes by the Bystander Test Group vs. Non-Bystander Test Group (boys)

The connection between the bystander behavior pattern of school bullying and the dysfunctional attitudes was revealed by linear regression analysis (stepwise method: dependant variable was the bystander behavior pattern, dysfunctional attitudes were used as predictors).

Chart 7 shows the results of linear regression analysis in case of bystander behavior pattern.

In case of the girls, bystander behavior pattern, from the dysfunctional attitudes, showed a significant, positive connection with need for affections and a negative one with external control-autonomy, which explained 7,6 % of the variance.

Predictor	B	t	P<
Women: $F_{totál}$=13,425; df=2/397; p<0,000			
Need for affections	0,161	3,205	0,001
External control - Autonomy	-0,159	-3,155	0,002

Chart 7. Correlation between the Attitudes that Might Become Dysfunctional with the Bystander Behaviour Pattern (approved models; p<0.05)

In case of the boys, bystander behavior pattern did not show significant, positive connection with any of the dysfunctional attitudes.

Predictor	B	t	P<
Keeping one's distance			
Women: $F_{totál}$=14,769; df=2/397; p<0,000			
Need for affections	0,195	3,846	0,000
External control - Autonomy	-0,165	-3,124	0,002
Fear			
Women: $F_{totál}$=7,028; df=1/397; p<0,008			
Need for affections	0,132	2,651	0,008

Chart 8. Regression Analysis of the Attitudes that Might Become Dysfunctional Versus the Individual Components of the Bystander Behaviour Pattern (approved models; p<0.05)

We also examined that what the connection is between the certain components of bystander behavior pattern (keeping one's distance, fear) and the dysfunctional attitudes (linear regression, stepwise method: dependant variable is the components of bystander behavior pattern, dysfunctional attitudes were used as predictors).

Chart 8 shows the revealed connections with this method.

In case of the girls, the keeping one's distance component of bystander behavior pattern, from the dysfunctional attitudes, showed a significant, positive connection with need for affections and a negative one with external control-autonomy, which explained 7,2 % of the variance.

In case of the boys, the keeping one's distance component of bystander behavior pattern did not show significant, positive connection with any of the dysfunctional attitudes.

In case of the girls, the fear component of bystander behavior pattern, from the dysfunctional attitudes, showed a significant, positive connection with need for affections, which explained 1,7 % of the variance.

In case of the boys, the fear component of bystander behavior pattern did not show significant, positive connection with any of the dysfunctional attitudes.

Coping Mechanisms

We examined what differences exist between the test groups in point of coping strategies on the basis of the results scored on the scale of the bystander behavior pattern' Questionnaire on School Bullying.

Figure 7 shows the averages scored on the certain scales of Conflict Solving Inventory of bystander vs. not bystander test groups in case of the girls.

Comparative Statistical Analysis shows that there were significant differences between the test groups in point of more coping strategies.

These are the following:

- Emotion focused coping strategy (t=3,650, p<0,000)
- Retrieval (t=3,449, p<0,001)
- Seeking emotional balance (t=3,040, p<0,003)
- Problem focused coping strategy (t=3,758, p<0,000)
- Conformance (t=3,670, p<0,000)
- Cognitive restructuring (t=2,845, p<0,005)

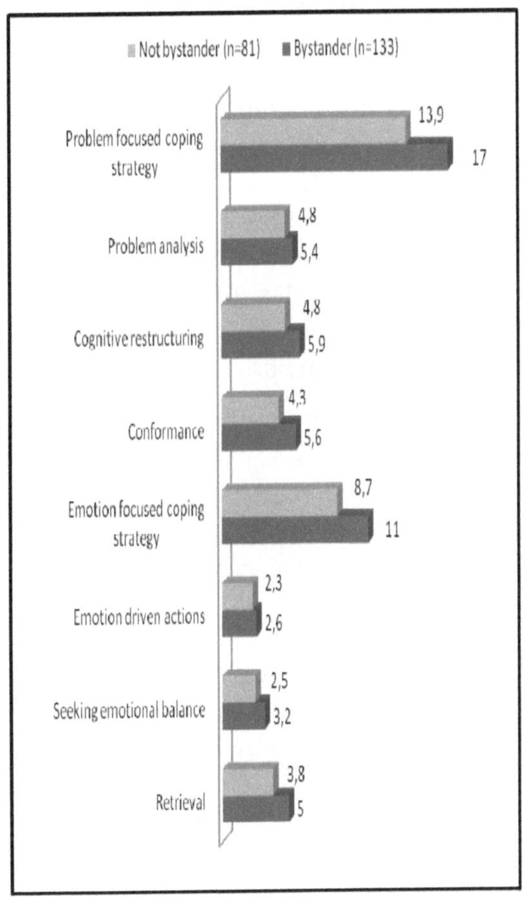

Figure 7. Averages Achieved on the Individual Scales of the Conflict Solving Inventory by the Bystander Test Group vs. Non- Bystander Test group (girls)

These results indicate that both the emotion focused coping strategies especially retrieval and seeking emotional balance and problem focused coping strategies especially conformance and cognitive restructuring were typical of the girls becoming bystanders of school bullying.

Figure 8 shows the averages scored on the certain scales of Conflict Solving Inventory of bystander vs. not bystander test groups in case of the boys.

Comparative Statistical Analysis (two-sample t-test) shows that there were significant differences between the test groups in point of more coping strategies.

These are the following:

- Emotion focused coping strategy (t=2,375, p<0,019)
- Seeking emotional balance (t=3,932, p<0,000)
- Retrieval (t=3,256, p<0,011)
- Problem focused coping strategy (t=3,431, p<0,001)
- Cognitive restructuring (t=3,322, p<0,001)
- Conformance (t=3,189, p<0,002)

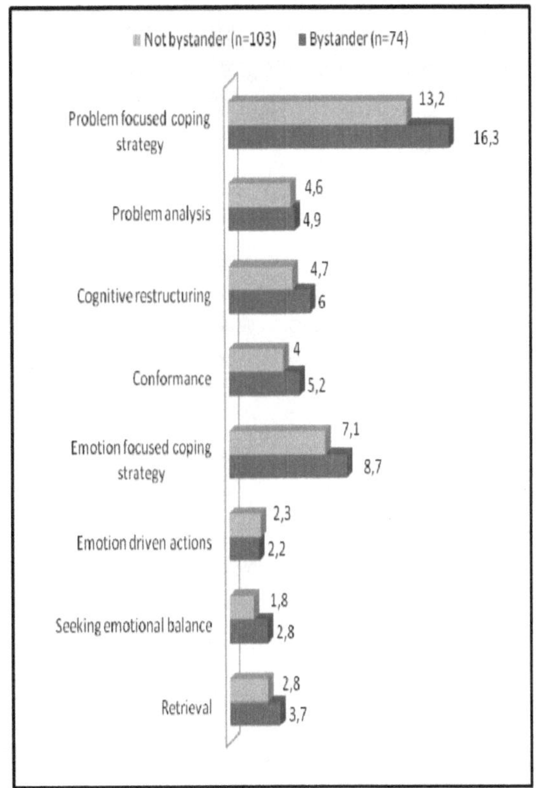

Figure 8. Averages Achieved on the Individual Scales of the Conflict Solving Inventory by the Bystander Test Group vs. Non- Bystander Test group (boys).

These results indicate that both the emotion focused coping strategies especially retrieval and seeking emotional balance and problem focused coping strategies especially conformance and cognitive restructuring were also typical of the boys becoming bystanders of school bullying.

The connection between the bystander behavior pattern of school bullying and the coping strategies was revealed by linear regression analysis (stepwise method: dependant variable was the bystander behavior pattern, coping strategies were used as predictors).

Chart 9 shows the results of linear regression analysis in case of bystander behavior pattern.

Predictor	B	t	P<
Women: $F_{totál}$=15,203; df=2/397; p<0,000			
Conformance	0,176	3,232	0,001
Retrieval	0,138	2,535	0,012
Men: $F_{totál}$=9,748; df=1/309; p<0,002			
Seeking emotional balance	0,175	3,122	0,002

Chart 9. Correlation of Conflict Solving Strategies with the Bystander Behaviour Pattern (approved models; p<0.05)

In case of the girls, bystander behavior pattern, from the coping strategies, showed a significant, positive connection with conformance and retrieval, which explained 7,2 % of the variance.

In case of the boys, bystander behavior pattern, from the coping strategies, showed a significant, positive connection with seeking emotional balance, which explained 3,1 % of the variance of bystander behavior pattern.

We also examined that what the connection is between the certain components of bystander behavior pattern (keeping one's distance, fear) and the coping strategies (linear regression, stepwise method: dependant variable is the components of bystander behavior pattern, coping strategies were used as predictors).

Chart 10 shows the revealed connections with this method.

Predictor	B	t	P<
Keeping one's distance			
Women: $F_{totál}$=153,803; df=2/397; p<0,000			
Conformance	0,199	3,668	0,001
Retrieval	0,111	2,048	0,041
Men: $F_{totál}$=11,444; df=1/309; p<0,000			
Seeking emotional balance	0,194	4,536	0,000

Fear			
Women: $F_{totál}$=7,723; df=1/397; p<0,006			
Retrieval	0,138	7,723	0,006
Men: $F_{totál}$=6,058; df=1/309; p<0,014			
Retrieval	0,137	2,461	0,014

Chart 10. Regression Analysis of Conflict Solving Strategies Versus the Individual Components of the Bystander Behaviour Pattern (approved models; p<0.05)

In case of the girls, the keeping one's distance component of bystander behavior pattern, from the coping strategies, showed a significant, positive connection with conformance and retrieval, which together explained 7,2 % of the variance.

In case of the boys, the keeping one's distance component of bystander behavior pattern, from the coping strategies, showed a significant, positive connection only with seeking emotional balance, which explained 3,1 % of the variance.

In case of the girls, the fear component of bystander behavior pattern, from the coping strategies, showed a significant, positive connection with retrieval, which together explained 1,9 % of the variance.

In case of the boys, the fear component of bystander behavior pattern, from the coping strategies, showed a significant, positive connection with retrieval, which together explained 2,1 % of the variance.

Discussion

In point of family socialization background effects, our research results show that from the behavior patterns of school bullying, bystander behavior pattern was the least of all in connection with family socialization effects. There was a difference between the socialization effects in case of the boys and the girls. Through school bullying the girls remain bystanders if one of their parents (no matter whether the father or the mother) is characterized by strong manipulative educational attitude. The boys are bystanders because of the paternal manipulative educational style associated with strict, punitive maternal educational style.

Examining the temperament and character traits, we found that bystander behavior pattern was more typical of the girls, and we could show only character traits as background effects. This behavior pattern - without reference to gender differences- was in close contact with the lack of cooperativeness. The bystander students of school bullying are not interested in others, are not helpful and they are socially intolerant. In case of this behavior pattern, the low value of the variance characterized by temperament and character traits indicates that there can be various socialization factors or other factors explained by group dynamics.

Our research results, which examine emotions, attitudes and coping, show that the students, who become bystanders through school bullying –without reference to gender differences-primarily, feel fear and shame. They cork up anger. Beside the above mentioned, retrieval and conformance coping strategy can be typical of the girls, who become bystanders.

Intensive need for affections is typical of them; they would like to be accepted by everybody as well as effort for autonomy is typical of them. Seeking emotional balance can be typical of the boys, who become bystanders.

References

Craig, W. M., Pepler, D., & Atlas, R. (2000). Observations of bullying in the playground in the classroom. *School Psychology International*, 21, 22-36.

Goch, I. (1998). *Entwicklung der Ungewissheitstoleranz. Die Bedeutung der familialen Socialization.* Regensburg: Roderer.

Izard, C.E. (1971): *The Face of Emotions.* Appleton-Century-Crofts, New York.

Figula E, Margitics F, Pauwlik Zs. (2019): *The Questionnaire on School Bullying /handbook/.* KeryPub. New York.

Kopp, M. (1994). *Orvosi pszichológia.* Budapest: SOTE Magatartástudományi Intézet.

Kopp, M., and Skrabski Á. (1995). *Alkalmazott magatartástudomány. [Applied behavioral science.]* Budapest: Corvinus Kiadó.

Margitics, F; Figula, E; Pauwlik, Zs (2010): *Prevalence of School Bullying in Hungarian Primary and High Schools.* KeryPub. New York.

O'Connell P, Pepler D, Craig W. Peer (1999): Involvement in bullying: Insights and challenges for intervention. *Journal Adolescence.* 1999;22(4):437-52.

Olweus, D. (1997). Täter-Opfer-Probleme in der Schule: Erkenntnisstand und Interventionsprogramm. In: Holtappels, H. G.; Heitmeyer, W.; Melzer, W.; Tillmann, K.-J. *Forschung über Gewalt an Schulen. Erscheinungsformen und Ursachen, Konzepte und Prävention.* Weinheim, München: Juventa Verlag.

Oláh, A. (2005): *Érzelmek, megküzdés és optimális élmény.* Trefor Kiadó, Budapest.

Raboteg-Saric Z., Bartakovic S. (2019): Empathy and Moral Disengagement as Predictors of Bystander Roles in School Bullying. *Paediatric Psychology*, 15(2):161-176.

Rózsa S., and Kállai, J., and Osváth, A., and Bánki M. Cs. (2005). *Temperamentum és karakter: Cloninger pszichobiológiai modellje. A Cloninger-féle temperamentum és karakter kérdőív felhasználói kézikönyve.* Budapest: Medicina

Sallay, H., and Dabert, C. (2002). Women's perception of parenting: a German-Hungarian comparison. *Applied Psychology in Hungary, 3-4*, 55-56.

Salmivalli, C., Lagerspetz, K., Björkqvist, K., Österman, K., Kaukiainen, A. (1996). Bullying as a group process: Participant roles and their relations to social status withinthe group. *Aggressive Behavior*, 22,1–15.

Swearer, S., and Hymel, S. (2015). Understanding the psychology of bullying: Moving toward a socialecological diathesis–stress model. *American Psychologist,* 70(4), 344–353.

Tani F, Greenman PS, Schneider BH, Fregoso M. (2003): A Study of childhood personality and participant roles in bullying incidents *School Psychol Int.* 24(2):131-46.

Thornberg, R., Jungert, T: (2013): Bystander behavior in bullying situations: basic moral sensitivity, moral disengagement and defender self-efficacy, *Journal of Adolescence,* (36), 3, 475-483.

Tóth, I., and Gervai, J. (1999). Szülői Bánásmód Kérdőív (H-PBI): a Parental Bonding Instrument magyar változata. *Magyar Pszichológiai Szemle, 54*, 551-566.

Weisman, A.N., and Beck, A.T. (1979). *The Dysfunctional Attitude Scale.* Thesis, University of Pennsylvania.